Stratigraphy of Lower to Middle Paleozoic Rocks of Northern Nevada and the Antler Orogeny

By Keith B. Ketner

Professional Paper 1799

U.S. Department of the Interior
U.S. Geological Survey

U.S. Department of the Interior
SALLY JEWELL, Secretary

U.S. Geological Survey
Suzette M. Kimball, Acting Director

U.S. Geological Survey, Reston, Virginia: 2013

For more information on the USGS—the Federal source for science about the Earth, its natural and living resources, natural hazards, and the environment, visit http://www.usgs.gov or call 1–888–ASK–USGS.

For an overview of USGS information products, including maps, imagery, and publications, visit http://www.usgs.gov/pubprod

To order this and other USGS information products, visit http://store.usgs.gov

Suggested citation:
Ketner, K.B., 2013, Stratigraphy of lower to middle Paleozoic rocks of northern Nevada and the Antler orogeny: U.S. Geological Survey Professional Paper 1799, 23 p., http://pubs.usgs.gov/pp/1799/.

Contents

Figures

Conversion Factors

SI to Inch/Pound

Multiply	By	To obtain
Length		
centimeter (cm)	0.3937	inch (in.)
millimeter (mm)	0.03937	inch (in.)
meter (m)	3.281	foot (ft)
kilometer (km)	0.6214	mile (mi)
kilometer (km)	0.5400	mile, nautical (nmi)
meter (m)	1.094	yard (yd)

Stratigraphy of Lower to Middle Paleozoic Rocks of Northern Nevada and the Antler Orogeny

By Keith B. Ketner

Abstract

Commonly accepted concepts concerning the lower Paleozoic stratigraphy of northern Nevada are based on the assumption that the deep-water aspects of Ordovician to Devonian siliceous strata are due to their origin in a distant oceanic environment, and their presence where we find them is due to tectonic emplacement by the Roberts Mountains thrust. The concept adopted here is based on the assumption that their deep-water aspects are the result of sea-level rise in the Cambrian, and all of the Paleozoic strata in northern Nevada are indigenous to that area. The lower part of the Cambrian consists mainly of shallow-water cross-bedded sands derived from the craton. The upper part of the Cambrian, and part of the Ordovician, consists mainly of deep-water carbonate clastics carried by turbidity currents from the carbonate shelf in eastern Nevada, newly constructed as a result of sea-level rise. Ordovician to mid-Devonian strata are relatively deep-water siliceous deposits, which are the western facies assemblage. The basal contact of this assemblage on autochthonous Cambrian rocks is exposed in three mountain ranges and is clearly depositional in all three. The western facies assemblage can be divided into distinct stratigraphic units of regional extent. Many stratigraphic details can be explained simply by known changes in sea level. Upper Devonian to Mississippian strata are locally and westerly derived orogenic clastic beds deposited disconformably on the western facies assemblage. This disconformity, clearly exposed in 10 mountain ranges, indicates regional uplift and erosion of the western facies assemblage and absence of local deformation. The disconformity represents the Antler orogeny.

Introduction

In Nevada, the north-trending Ordovician to Devonian carbonate shelf gives way westward to the western facies assemblage—an expanse of dark, siliceous sedimentary rocks and sparse volcanic rocks dotted with small bodies of carbonate shelf strata (fig. 1; Stewart 1980).

The western facies assemblage in northern Nevada, the Cambrian strata that underlie it, and the Upper Devonian to

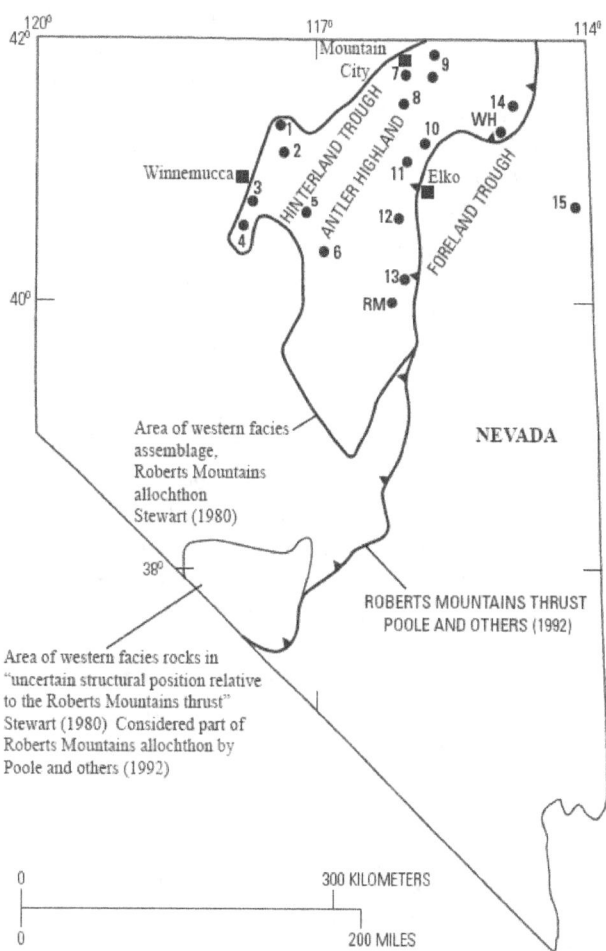

Figure 1. Index map of Nevada showing the Roberts Mountains allochthon and Roberts Mountains thrust as conventionally conceived. The outlined areas are the western facies domain of this report. Numbered localities correspond to the numbered columns in figure 2.1–Hot Springs Range, 2–Osgood Mountains, 3–Sonoma Range, 4–East Range, 5–Battle Mountain (also the town), 6–Northern Shoshone Range, 7–Northern Bull Run Mountains, 8–Northern Independence Mountains, 9–Rowland-Rosebud Mountain (Rowland is the northern dot), 10–Northern Adobe Range, 11–Southern Independence Mountains, 12–Northern Piñon Range, 13–Northern Sulphur Spring Range, 14–HD Range, 15–Goshute-Toano Range. RM–Roberts Mountains, WH–Windermere Hills.

Mississippian orogenic deposits that overlie it are the subject of this report. The western facies assemblage is commonly thought to constitute the Roberts Mountains allochthon and to have been "obducted" onto the carbonate shelf from an oceanic or back-arc basin located far to the west (Burchfiel and others, 1992; Miller and others, 1992; Poole and others, 1992; Crafford, 2008; and references in each). The scattered small bodies of Middle Cambrian to Devonian carbonate shelf rocks within the domain of the western facies assemblage are generally thought to be exposures of shelf rocks in windows of the allochthon. I offered an alternative hypothesis (Ketner, 2012), which stated that Cambrian rocks and the western facies assemblage were deposited essentially in situ, and the scattered bodies of Ordovician to Devonian shelf rocks were slide blocks resulting from collapse of the shelf and transported by gravity into the western facies domain. The present report is based on this hypothesis and on the concept that the deep-water aspects of the Cambrian and Ordovician calcareous turbidites and the Ordovician to Devonian western facies assemblage are due to sea-level rise in the Cambrian.

The structure of the lower to middle Paleozoic rocks is extremely complex, due mainly to Pennsylvanian and younger tectonism (Ketner, 1977, 1984, 1998b, 2008, 2012; Ketner and Alpha, 1992; Trexler and others, 2004), but most of the stratigraphic components have been partially dated by fossils to the extent that the stratigraphy in many areas can be pieced together with considerable confidence. Moreover, many critical exposures of contacts have been observed and mapped (fig. 2). The western facies assemblage is underlain depositionally by Cambrian carbonate rocks. It has a regionally consistent internal stratigraphy and is overlain disconformably by mainly Upper Devonian and Mississippian rocks. The scope of this report includes the lower to middle Paleozoic sequence in the western facies assemblage of 14 mountain ranges of northern Nevada, notable stratigraphic and lithic features, and the nature of the Antler orogeny. This report is based on intensive field studies that I have undertaken in all of the mountain ranges named in figure 2.

Conventionally, the term western facies assemblage includes only siliceous Ordovician to Devonian relatively deep-water deposits, and that is how the term is used here. However, it should be understood that Cambrian to mid-Ordovician calcareous turbidites and debris flows are relatively deep-water deposits also.

In this report, the term "disconformity" is a sedimentary gap representing an erosional interval without evidence of local deformation—the bedding planes above and below it are parallel.

An extensive collection of thin sections of several formations described in this report are archived in the U.S. Geological Survey Library in Denver, Colorado. They are organized under my name, primarily by specific geologic map areas and secondarily by stratigraphic units.

Sea-Level Rise in the Early Paleozoic

The underlying concept adopted here is that the deep-water aspects of the western facies assemblage are the result of sea-level rise (fig. 3). The continental sedimentary sequences of Sloss (1963) are relevant to the stratigraphy of Nevada as indicated also by Finney and Perry (1991). These sequences are based on advances and retreats of shorelines across the continent through the Paleozoic. The significance for Nevada is that the sea deepened beginning in Middle Cambrian to a maximum near the Cambrian-Ordovician boundary, shallowed briefly in the Ordovician, and deepened again to a maximum near the Ordovician-Silurian boundary. The deepening of the sea, beginning in the Cambrian, implies that the presence of the deep-water western facies assemblage in Nevada can be explained by eastward advance of facies boundaries, rather than by the eastward emplacement of an allochthon. Many stratigraphic details of the western facies assemblage can be explained by known changes in sea level as related in subsequent sections.

The Stratigraphic Sequence

Strata described here include Cambrian rocks, Ordovician to Devonian rocks of the western facies assemblage, and the orogenic rocks that directly overlie that assemblage (fig. 2). References are held to a minimum here; sources of data and details of stratigraphy are given in the appendix.

Although obscured by complex structure and chaotic nomenclature, the lower to middle Paleozoic stratigraphy of northern Nevada is remarkably uniform. The lower part of the Cambrian sequence consists mainly of shallow-water cross-bedded sands derived from the craton. The upper part of the Cambrian and part of the Ordovician consists mainly of deep-water carbonate clastics carried by turbidity currents and debris flows from the carbonate shelf in eastern Nevada, newly constructed as a result of sea-level rise. Ordovician to mid-Devonian strata are relatively deep-water siliceous deposits—the western facies assemblage—which can be subdivided into stratigraphic subdivisions of regional extent. Upper Devonian to Mississippian strata are locally and westerly derived orogenic clastic beds deposited on the western facies assemblage with a contact that is clearly disconformable. The disconformity represents the Antler orogeny.

Lower to Lower Middle Cambrian Units

The Osgood Mountain and Prospect Mountain Quartzites are the principal subjects of this section. The names are synonymous, and they refer to a very widespread sheet of quartzitic sandstone that was deposited across northern Nevada and reaches far into the continental interior (Sloss, 1963; Seeland, 1968; Lochman-Balk, 1972). The sandstone lies, with an indefinite contact, on siliceous rocks of Proterozoic age, and it could, therefore, be partly of Precambrian age.

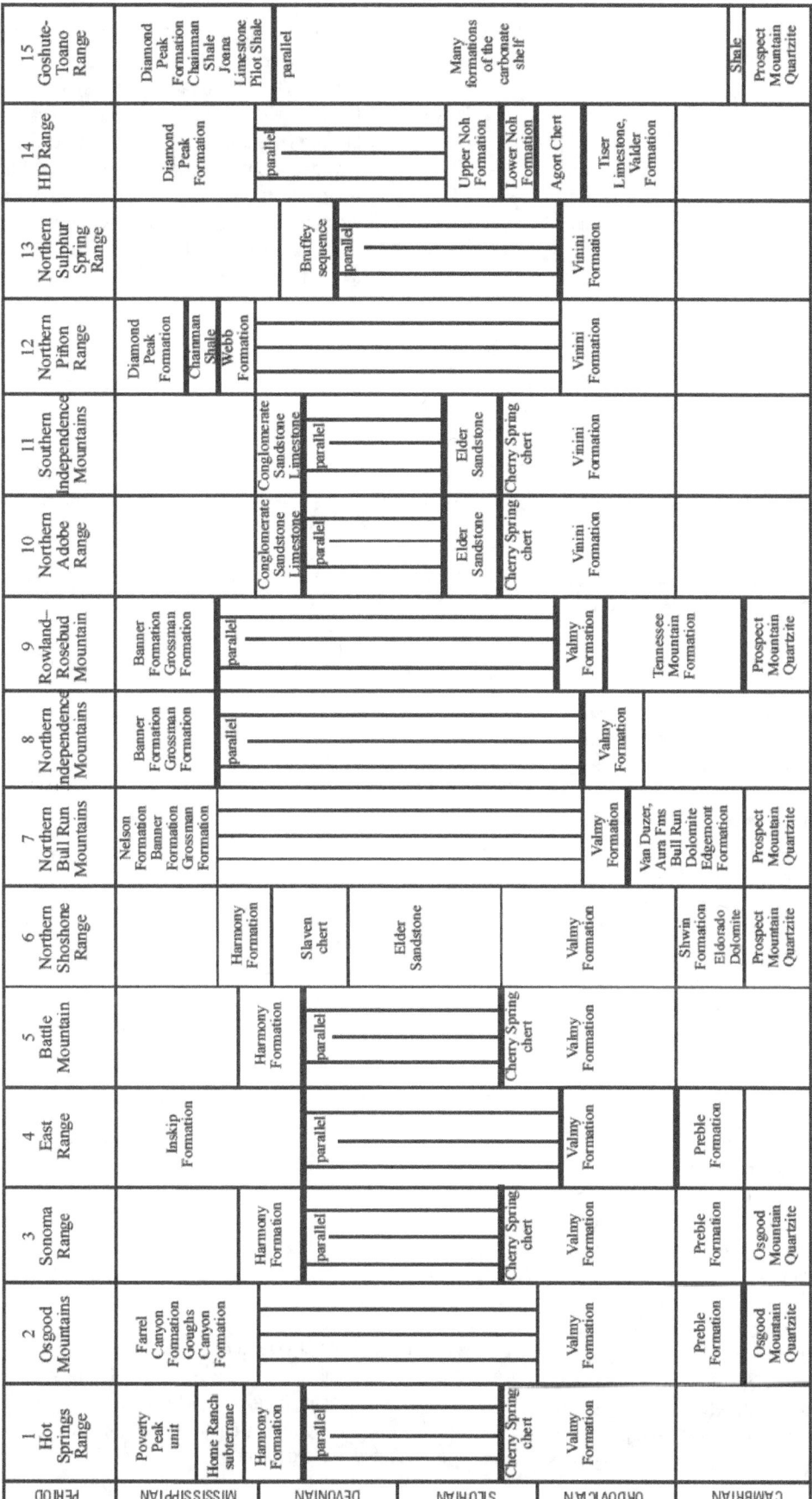

Figure 2. Stratigraphic columns of lower to mid-Paleozoic strata assembled partly on the basis of observed contacts and partly on the basis of their ages. With the exception of column 15, all of the columns represent stratigraphic relations of the western facies assemblage. Columns 1–5 are in the hinterland trough; columns 7–14 are within the Antler uplifted area; column 6 is marginal; column 15, included for comparison, is in the foreland trough. Heavy horizontal lines indicate sedimentary contacts that are exposed and were observed. The word "parallel" in most columns indicates that bedding, in the units above and below, was determined to be essentially parallel by direct observation, map relations, or both—elsewhere, the attitude of beds near the contact could not be determined accurately. The stratigraphic gap, indicated by vertical lines, between lower Paleozoic rocks and Devonian to Mississippian units represents uplift and erosion during the Antler orogeny. Column 15 represents conditions in the Antler foreland trough where there was no significant erosion before deposition of the orogenic sediments in the Late Devonian and Mississippian.

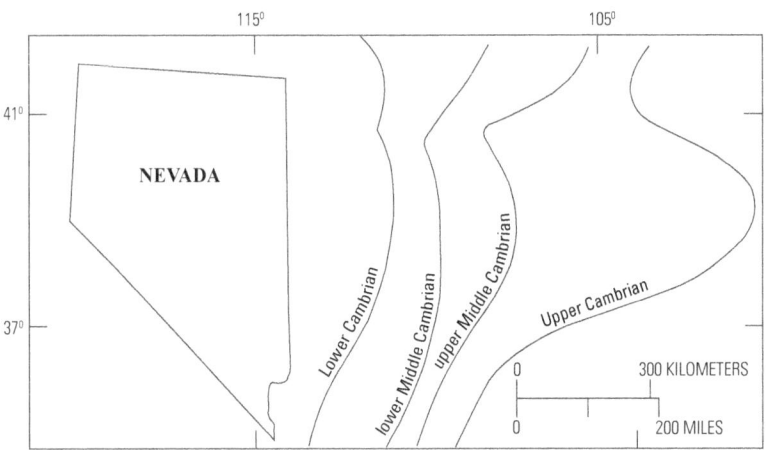

Figure 3. Shorelines in the Cambrian showing eastward advance through the Cambrian. This resulted in deepening of the sea in Nevada, which, in turn, caused the boundary between shallow- and deep-water facies to advance eastward (after Lochman-Balk, 1972). Accordingly, the presence of the deep-water western facies assemblage in Nevada can be explained by sedimentary processes rather than by contractional tectonics.

In some localities (fig. 2, columns 2, 6, 7, and 9), the quartzite includes at its top, or is overlain by, shaley beds correlated to the Pioche Shale of the east-central shelf sequence (Nolan and others, 1956). In two of these localities (fig. 2, columns 6 and 7), the shaley beds are overlain by dolomite identified as the Cambrian Eldorado Dolomite. These beds of shale and dolomite at the boundary between Lower and Middle Cambrian were deposited broadly on Cambrian sandstone at the onset of sea-level rise. Although they are considered a part of the carbonate shelf, the shale and dolomite beds extended much farther west than younger members of the shelf, and their relatively wide distribution is due to original deposition. This contrasts with Ordovician to Devonian carbonate bodies in the western facies domain which are considered to be slide blocks due to shelf collapse in the Devonian (Ketner, 2012).

The quartzite is well exposed in and near the Osgood Mountains (Hotz and Willden, 1964), in the Bull Run Mountains (Ehman, 1985), and at Rosebud Mountain (Ketner, 2007). In those areas, the quartzite is composed mainly of fine- to coarse-grained quartz sandstone and sporadic small-pebble conglomerate. Strata in the formation are typically crossbedded, and the orientation of the crossbedding conforms to the regional pattern of generally east to west depositional currents (fig. 4).

Lower to lower Middle Cambrian exposures in northern Nevada are assumed to be autochthonous because they are not known to be underlain by faults, their lithic composition is similar to correlative strata underlying the shelf sequence, and the direction of crossbedding in quartzite conforms to the regional pattern as shown in figure 4.

Certain sedimentary features of the Osgood Mountain Quartzite contrast with those of Ordovician quartzites, and those differences point to a different source of sand and a distinctly different environment of deposition. According to Hotz and Willden (1964), the main body of the Osgood Mountain Quartzite is composed generally of fine- to medium-grained quartz and contains a very small percentage of feldspar and chert grains. Those authors reported sporadic, uncommon pebbles with diameters of as much as 8 mm. In the present study, grains of as much as 2 mm in diameter were observed but are uncommon. Representative texture and range of grain size are shown in figure 5.

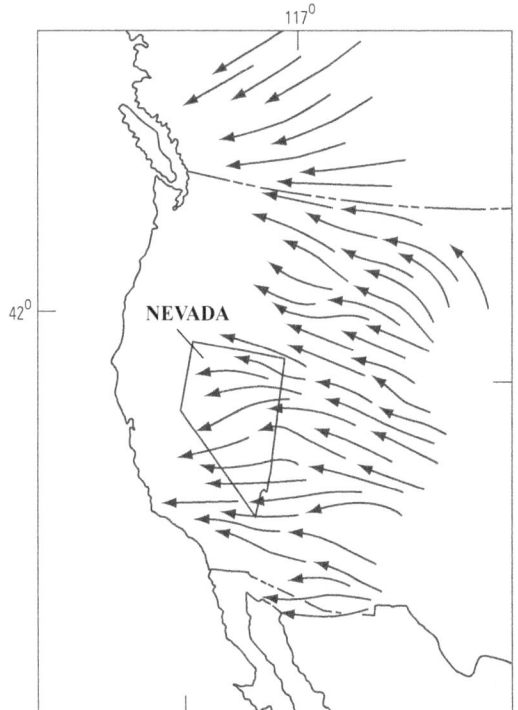

Figure 4. Western North America showing trend lines of currents in Cambrian sandstone determined from crossbedding (Seeland, 1968). Crossbedding in the Osgood Mountains and elsewhere in Nevada contributed to the dataset.

Figure 5. Osgood Mountain Quartzite, Osgood Mountains, illustrating a texture of sutured grain boundaries, poor sorting, and common grain-size range, all of which contrast with the texture of Ordovician quartzites (compare with fig. 6) (crossed polarizers).

Mid-Cambrian to Mid-Ordovician Calcareous Turbidites and Debris Flows

The Preble and Tennessee Mountain Formations and their partial correlatives such as the Shwin, Van Duzer, and Aura Formations, are the subject of this section. Due to deepening of the sea in mid-Cambrian time, a carbonate shelf was constructed in eastern Nevada and Utah on Lower to Middle Cambrian rocks (Lochman-Balk, 1972). This restricted the source of sand and supplied a source of detrital calcareous debris. Calcareous sediments of the Preble and Tennessee Mountain Formations were derived from the carbonate shelf as it grew and were deposited largely by turbidity currents and debris flows (Rees and Rowell, 1980) in the deepening water of northern Nevada. The base of the Preble-Tennessee Mountain sequence is depositional and conformable with Cambrian quartzite as exposed in the Osgood Mountains (Hotz and Willden, 1964) and at Rosebud Mountain (Ketner, 2007). Greenstone is present in these formations, especially near their contact with the overlying Valmy Formation, and barite deposits are present in the Preble Formation.

Western Facies Assemblage

As the sea continued to deepen, and the carbonate shelf continued to build up, siliceous and carbonate sediments accumulated in northern Nevada from Early Ordovician to Devonian as detailed in following sections. These deposits, the western facies assemblage, are composed largely of bedded chert, limestone, shale, siltstone, sandstone, including pure quartzite, and conglomerate. In addition, the assemblage includes sporadic small bodies of basaltic greenstone, scattered deposits of stratiform barite, and, in the Ordovician and Silurian, deposits of sulfides. Sulfide deposits appear to be confined to the western facies assemblage, but basalt and barite deposits are also present in the underlying Cambrian rocks and in the overlying orogenic formations.

Most of the sedimentary rocks are dark from the presence of organic matter, and they generally lack an indigenous shelly fauna. In the East Range, the lowermost beds were dated by means of conodonts near the Cambrian-Ordovician boundary (J.E. Repetski cited in Ketner and others, 2000); in the Rowland-Rosebud Mountain area, the boundary was dated by conodonts as Middle Ordovician (Ketner and others, 1995).

Ordovician to Lower Silurian Rocks

In Nevada, the terms Valmy Formation and Vinini Formation are customarily applied to relatively deep-water strata of known Ordovician age. However, the Vinini includes the informal Lower Silurian Cherry Spring chert in several localities (Noble and Finney, 1999), and I have observed the Cherry Spring chert in both the Vinini and Valmy Formations in other places. Although the Valmy has been displaced partly or entirely by low-angle faults in much of Nevada, and is commonly regarded as entirely allochthonous, it clearly lies with gradational, depositional contacts on the autochthonous Preble Formation in the East Range and on the autochthonous Tennessee Mountain Formation or equivalents in both the Bull Run Mountains and the Rowland-Rosebud Mountain area (fig. 2; Ketner and others, 1993, 1995, 2000).

Both the Valmy and Vinini Formations are composed mainly of shale, siltstone, sandstone, quartzite, bedded chert, limestone, and greenstone. However, there are important differences; the Vinini includes relatively little quartzite and greenstone but relatively more heterogeneous sandstone and limestone. It also includes dolomite, and graptolites are much more abundant. The Vinini is present generally east of exposures of the Valmy and appears to be a more inboard, shallower facies. Because the Vinini is relatively fossiliferous and has been investigated in considerable detail, its internal lithic and stratigraphic features can be determined as described previously (Ketner, 1991) and summarized here. The informal members of the Vinini discussed below have counterparts in the type Vinini of the Roberts Mountains as described by Finney and Perry (1991) and Noble (2000).

The lower member of the Vinini, of Early to Middle Ordovician age, consists of rocks that are more coarse grained and more calcareous than those of younger beds. Attributes of turbidity current deposits, such as graded bedding, are displayed by some arenite beds, but others are entirely devoid of such features. The sequence of beds in this part of the Vinini is randomly varied in thickness, composition, texture, and sedimentary structures reflecting a constantly changing environment. Sand-size detrital components form the bulk of the lower member and conglomerates are common. These features can be ascribed to a relatively low stand of sea level in the early part of the Ordovician (Sloss, 1963; Finney and Perry, 1991). Except for quartzite, most arenites are extremely heterogeneous in composition.

The heterogeneous arenites, whether calcareous or siliceous, are composed of generally poorly sorted and poorly rounded clasts. Components of the arenites are (1) quartz sand; (2) calcareous fragments of pelmatozoans, trilobites, gastropods, cephalopods, ostracodes, brachiopods, and the alga *Nuia*; (3) phosphatic fragments of the crustacean *Caryocaris*, inarticulate brachiopods, and conodonts; (4) sponge spicules, both siliceous and calcareous; (5) calcareous fecal pellets; (6) dolomite rhombs and glauconite grains; and (7) rock fragments including dolomite, limestone, shale, and chert. In addition, some clasts consist of limestone slabs that have been ripped up and rotated. Some of these are as much as 0.5 m in diameter.

Many chert beds in the lower member of the Vinini are pseudo-cherts. They resemble normal bedded chert in the outcrop, but under the microscope, they are seen to be sandstones composed of siliceous spicules, chert grains, dolomite rhombs, and miscellaneous debris. This kind of chert is commonly associated with detrital dolomite and, in places, grades into dolomite. Pseudo-chert contrasts with cherts of the middle to upper members of the Vinini, which are ordinary bedded cherts nearly free of clasts and organic remains. Iron, zinc, and lead sulfides occur sporadically in the lower Middle Ordovician part of the Vinini (Ketner, 1983, 1991).

Strata associated with the heterogeneous arenites and conglomerates are pure quartz sandstone and quartzite and limestone beds composed almost entirely of calcareous components such as pellets and fragments of *Nuia*. Other strata include shale and siltstone and radiolarian-bearing, nondetrital bedded chert. Greenstone is a minor component.

The middle member of the Vinini, of Middle to Late Ordovician age, is more uniform stratigraphically, and lithic units have more lateral continuity than those of the lower member. It is generally finer grained than the lower member, reflecting a deepening of the sea in the later part of the Ordovician. Although it is composed mainly of carbonaceous shale, it also includes micritic limestone, mature quartz sandstone or quartzite, and chert. Chert beds of the middle member contain radiolarians or other spheroidal skeletons; however, these are a minor constituent, and most of the chert is free of any sign of organic remains and free of clastic components. Sparse quartzite beds are composed wholly of quartz. Graptolites are abundant in the shale and constitute the principal macroscopic indigenous fauna of the middle member. The limestone beds are black micrites composed almost entirely of calcareous spicules and calcispheres.

The upper member of the Vinini is a conspicuous chert couplet composed of a lower black chert unit and an upper white chert unit deposited during maximum sea level at the Ordovician-Silurian boundary. This member is discussed in a subsequent section (Chert Couplet at the Ordovician-Silurian Boundary). There are remarkably similar counterparts to the Vinini Formation in Arkansas and Texas where Lower

to Middle Ordovician sandy, conglomeratic beds are overlain mainly by Middle to Upper Ordovician shale, which is overlain by conspicuous black, bedded chert overlain at the Ordovician-Silurian boundary (in Texas) by white chert (King, 1937; Ketner, 1980 and references therein).

Ordovician Quartzite

Quartzite of the Valmy and Vinini Formations differs lithicly from that of the Osgood Mountain and Prospect Mountain Quartzites in its smaller maximum grain size, much better sorting, greater purity, association with bedded chert, absence of sedimentary structures, and occurrence as relatively thick beds. One such bed, measured in the northern Independence Mountains, is more than 30 m thick. The Ordovician quartzite throughout north-central Nevada is extremely pure at more than 96 percent SiO_2 (Ketner, 1966). The remaining percentage is mainly interstitial carbonate and carbonate veinlets.

The quartzite commonly occurs as multiple beds of pure quartz separated by shale, argillite, chert, and greenstone. Because the Valmy is a relatively deep-water stratigraphic unit, it is tempting to assume the detrital components would be graded and to attribute their deposition to turbidity currents. However, in the type section of the Valmy, the usual hallmarks of turbidity-current deposits are conspicuously absent. Chert, shale, and quartzite are randomly interbedded with abrupt contacts. The quartzite beds are even-grained with maximum grain size of about 1 mm (figs. 6 and 7).

Figure 6.   Type Valmy Formation, Battle Mountain, showing top of 3-m bed of quartzite (crossed polarizers). This specimen has typical texture including an isolated grain distinctly larger than average. The maximum diameter of such grains is about 1.2 mm based on examination of hundreds of thin sections from many localities across northern Nevada (Ketner, 1966). Compare with typical Cambrian quartzite of figure 5.

Figure 7. Type Valmy Formation, Battle Mountain, showing base of the same bed as shown in figure 6. These two figures are typical of tops and bases of massive quartzite beds in the region. Invariably they show lack of gradation in grain size from base to top. All of the grains are quartz.

Figure 8. Type Valmy Formation, Battle Mountain, showing bedded chert sequence between massive quartzite beds. The card is about 12 cm wide.

Figure 9. Type Valmy Formation, Battle Mountain, showing the smooth underside of a quartzite bed. This is typical of quartzite beds in the area.

In a well-exposed part of the type area of the Valmy Formation, on Battle Mountain, west of Trout Creek (Roberts, 1964), shale is present sporadically, but some quartzite beds are intimately interbedded solely with chert. The chert intervals appear to be normal bedded cherts like any other. Because an association of bedded chert and quartz-ite seems an unlikely and illogical combination, this part of the sequence was observed closely. Figure 8 shows one of several such successions. The well-exposed undersides of all of the quartzite beds at this locality are slightly undulating or perfectly planar, smooth, and devoid of fluting, groove marks, load casts, and trace fossils (fig. 9). The contacts of quartzite beds with overlying chert beds are abrupt without the slightest gradation interval or trace of shale.

The depositional conditions of the Valmy and Vinini quartzite beds are problematic. The associated strata of bedded chert and graptolitic shale, together with dark color and absence of a shelly fauna, constitute a suite that is usually considered to have been deposited in relatively deep water. Deposition by turbidity currents would seem to be an option, but the lack of typical features of turbidite deposits raises questions about the depositional environment. The lack of grading could be explained by relatively uniform grain size in the source area, but the depositional conditions of ungraded beds of pure quartz sand lacking sole marks, abruptly alternat-ing with bedded chert, is an unsolved problem.

The geographic source of quartz sand that makes up pure sandstone and quartzite beds of the Valmy and Vinini is controversial. Some of the beds are approximately correlative with the Eureka Quartzite of the shelf area, and it is tempting to regard them as spillage from the shelf into deeper water in which the Valmy Formation was deposited (Miller and Larue,

1983; Finney and Perry, 1991). However, a genetic connection is questionable because (1) the Vinini Formation, almost lack-ing in quartzite in most places, lies between the Eureka and the Valmy Formation where most of the quartzite is concentrated; (2) quartz sand grains of the Valmy appear to be slightly larger on average, and less well-sorted, than those of the Eureka (Ketner, 1966); (3) although the ages of some quartzite beds in the western facies assemblage are claimed to be close to that of the Eureka (Finney and Perry, 1991), the ages of quartzite beds in the Valmy Formation are very difficult to establish owing to poorly exposed contacts and scarcity of fossils. Much more work is required before a close correlation between the Eureka Quartzite and quartzites of the Valmy and Vinini Formations is proved.

Chert Couplet at the Ordovician-Silurian Boundary

A distinctive chert couplet constitutes the uppermost beds of both the Valmy and Vinini Formations as observed at several locations in the area of this report (fig. 2), in southern Nevada, northern Mexico, and elsewhere (Ketner, 1998b). This couplet consists essentially of a lower black chert unit a few meters thick, and an upper, mainly white, chert unit a few meters thick. Shale and thin chert beds are present in the sequence at locally variable stratigraphic levels. The black chert is Late Ordovician age as indicated by graptolite collections in the Adobe Range (Ketner and Ross, 1990), the HD Range (Riva, 1970), in northern Mexico (Riva and Ketner, (1989), and elsewhere (Ketner, 1998b). The white chert is Early Silurian age as indicated by radiolarians identified at several localities (Noble and Finney, 1999). Noble and others (1997) informally designated the upper unit as the Cherry Spring chert where it is well exposed in the northern Adobe Range. This remarkable couplet of relatively pure chert was deposited when the sea extended across North America (Sloss, 1963), and in Nevada, it presumably was at maximum depth.

The black chert component of the couplet appears to be quite normal for Middle to Upper Ordovician western facies bedded chert in Nevada—dark chert beds separated by shaly seams. In many localities, however, the chert beds tend to be unusually thick. Microscopically it has a normal texture of interlocking, usually distinctly visible, quartz grains, scattered radiolarian-like or spore-like objects, and a significant content of dark organic matter. Like most bedded chert in the western facies assemblage, it is brittle and breaks into blocky fragments. Graptolites are commonly embedded in the chert.

The white chert unit is unique in the western facies assemblage. It is normally white or very light gray and most beds are a meter or more thick (figs. 10, 11, and 12). Microscopically it is consistently very fine grained. Radiolarian-like or spore-like bodies are very scarce; in most thin sections observed, they are totally absent; no spicules were observed. Unlike ordinary bedded cherts, most of the unit is coherent and breaks conchoidally. Locally, the white chert is porous, and the porous parts of the rock are commonly stained with green and brown iron minerals. In the more intensely stained exposures, the rock is a collapse breccia (fig. 13). This staining and the breccia appear to be due to oxidation and solution of pyrite and other sulfides. The phenomenon is so widespread and is so characteristic of this particular stratigraphic unit that the occurrence of sulfides must be contemporaneous with deposition and not due to solutions emanating from local intrusive rocks of distinctly younger ages. Galena has been

Figure 10.   Cherry Spring chert where it is well exposed in northern Adobe Range. Lower Silurian, thick-bedded white chert at the top of the Vinini Formation (Ketner and Ross, 1990; Noble and others, 1997). Hammer for scale.

Figure 11.   Cherry Spring chert, Cerro Cobachi, Sonora, Mexico. Thick-bedded white chert overlying thick-bedded black chert (Ketner and Noll, 1987). The white chert is altered to strongly pigmented, porous gossan in places. The underlying thick-bedded black chert was dated by graptolites as Late Ordovician (Riva and Ketner, 1989). Hammer for scale.

mined from this unit in the Adobe Range, and I have observed both galena and sphalerite in outcrops. Some samples contain anomalously high amounts of silver (Ketner, 1983).

The chert couplet occurs widely in the western facies domain of Nevada and was identified in a displaced terrane in Sonora, Mexico (Ketner and Noll, 1987). A similar couplet occurs in Texas as the upper part of the Maravillas Formation (Upper Ordovician shale and thick-bedded black chert; King, 1937) overlain by the lower part of the Caballos Novaculite (Lower Silurian, thick-bedded white chert; King, 1937; Noble, 1994). The distinctive appearance and widespread nature of

Figure 12. Chert couplet, Grand Trunk Canyon, Sonoma Range. Black chert, lower left; Lower Silurian Cherry Spring chert, center; clastic unit at the base of the Havallah sequence, upper right.

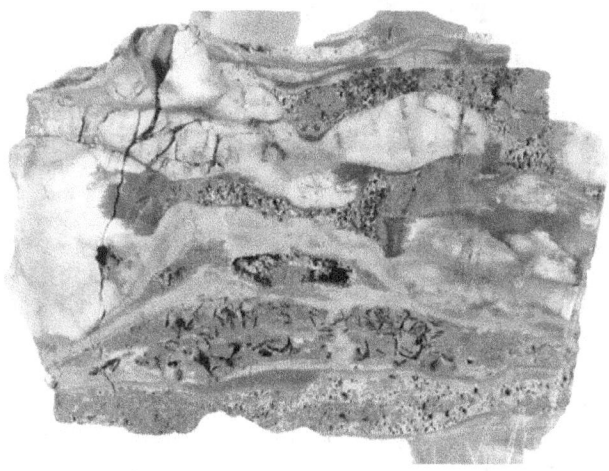

Figure 13. Lower Silurian Cherry Spring chert at the top of the Vinini Formation, Northern Adobe Range. Local sulfide deposits in the chert have oxidized producing a porous gossan of collapse breccia and intense blue-green and brown staining. The specimen is about 12 cm wide.

the couplet unites the Valmy and Vinini Formations because it is at the top of each and provides a conspicuous lithic marker horizon for regional physical correlation in the western facies domain.

Silurian and Devonian Sandstone

In some areas, the Elder Sandstone of Middle Silurian to Early Devonian age overlies the Cherry Spring chert (fig. 2). The Middle Silurian age has been widely reported; the Early Devonian age was reported by Noble (2000). Quartz clasts constitute most of this member, but feldspar and muscovite are abundant. Other strata consist of black to commonly

light-colored bedded chert, pure quartz sandstone, siltstone, and shale. Bedding surfaces commonly are covered by meandering trails, and graptolites are preserved on a few surfaces. In many exposures, the unit appears to be a distal turbidite. The unit resembles the approximately correlative Blaylock Sandstone of Arkansas and Oklahoma in its feldspar and mica content and in its turbidite features (Ketner, 1980 and references therein).

Middle and Upper Devonian Rocks

Middle Devonian conodonts have been identified in rocks in the northern Adobe Range (Ketner and Ross, 1990) and northern Sulphur Spring Range (this report). These collections are sparse, occur in detrital limestone, and are suspected of being reworked as described in the appendix. Middle and Late Devonian fossils from the Slaven Chert in the Shoshone Range have been reported (see appendix), but the kinds of strata associated with their occurrence have not been described in detail. As a result it is impossible to assign the associated strata to the pre-Antler or post-Antler sequences. More detailed stratigraphic work needs to be done in the Shoshone Range to resolve this problem.

Middle Ordovician Bioherm of the Adobe Range

A unique type of limestone is present in the northern Adobe Range. Conspicuous bodies of extremely fossiliferous shallow-water limestone are arrayed east-west among rocks of the western facies assemblage and orogenic deposits (Ketner and Ross, 1990). The aligned, erosional remnants extend 10 km across the Adobe Range and also are present, on strike, in the southern Independence Mountains 25 km to the west. These can be interpreted as remnants of a single extensive bioherm. The bioherm, which was dated as early Middle Ordovician by means of conodonts (J.E. Repetski, USGS, written commun., 2002) overlies Upper Devonian rocks on a low-angle fault that is parallel to bedding above and below. It is overlain disconformably by graptolite-bearing Lower Silurian black chert and siltstone. This contact appears to be a karst-like or crevassed surface because the Silurian graptolitic chert occupies crevices and deep hollows in the surface of the bioherm.

Parts of the bioherm display an obscure large-scale (bouldery) fragmental structure that is interpreted to be a normal reef-like, shallow-water feature contemporaneous with the buildup of the bioherm. The bioherm displays indistinct internal bedding parallel to the upper and lower surfaces. It consists of the following components, not necessarily in order of abundance, which has not been determined accurately: (1) fossil fragments identified as gastropods, pelecypods, brachiopods, trilobites, ostracodes, crinoid columnals, and conodonts (fig. 14); (2) abundant fragments of the alga *Nuia* (fig. 15); (3) clear spar some of which is interpreted as echinodermal plates; (4) pellets assumed to be fecal (fig. 16); (5) radiaxial fibrous calcite or stromatactis (fig. 17);. (6) fine-grained carbonate; and (7) spar with inclusions, interpreted as secondary calcite. These components ally the bioherm with the lower member of the Vinini, but the bioherm is pure bioclastic limestone free from quartz sand and exotic rock fragments. Other than the bioherm, no lower Paleozoic carbonate facies rocks are exposed in the northern Adobe Range.

A well-described lithically similar body correlative with the bioherm is present in southern Nevada—the Meiklejohn Peak "mudmound" (Ross and others, 1975). Unlike the Adobe

bioherm, it lies in stratigraphic continuity within a shallow-water shelf sequence. And, unlike the Adobe Range bioherm, the mudmound has a "zebra" textured basal component. If such a component had existed at the base of the bioherm, it was separated from the biohermal part by the fault that underlies it.

The history of the bioherm defies a simple explanation, and two possible explanations are offered. The preferred explanation is (1) it originated on the carbonate shelf in the early Middle Ordovician; (2) it was elevated and a karst-like surface developed; (3) it was deeply depressed, or was displaced into deep water in the Silurian, received a blanket of deep-water sediments; and (4) with its Silurian cap, it was then tectonically emplaced on Devonian strata in the Late Devonian or later.

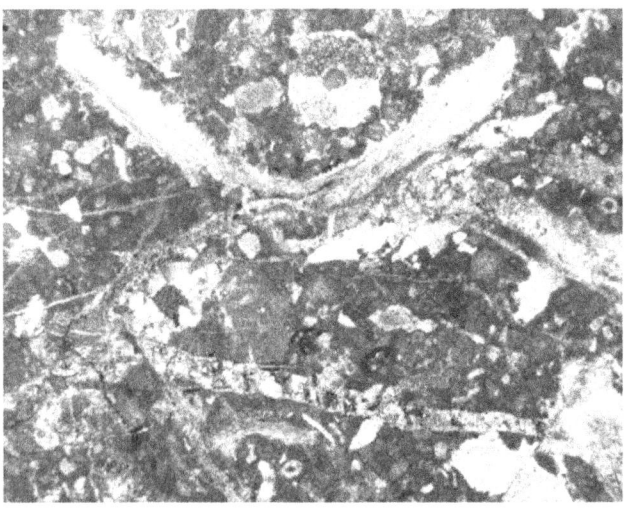

Figure 14. Ordovician bioherm, Adobe Range, showing shell fragments embedded in micrite (crossed polarizers).

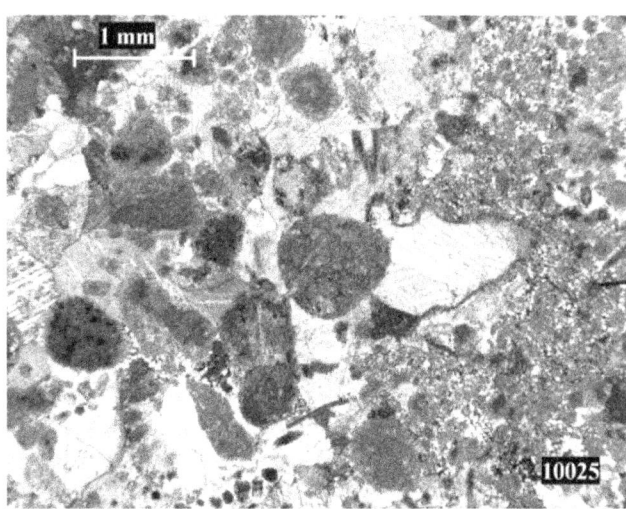

Figure 16. Ordovician bioherm, Adobe Range, showing large and small calcite pellets and sparry calcite, all cemented with fine-grained quartz mosaic. Dark color of pellets due to organic matter (crossed polarizers).

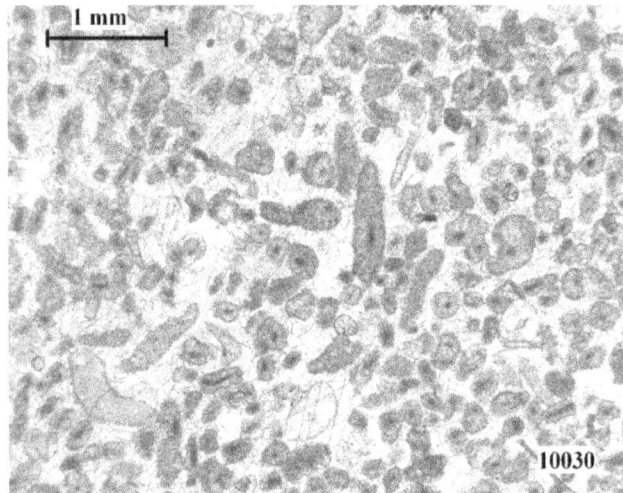

Figure 15. Ordovician bioherm, Adobe Range, showing fragments of the alga *Nuia* cemented by mosaic of sparry calcite and quartz (uncrossed polarizers).

Figure 17. Ordovician bioherm, Adobe Range, showing radiaxial calcite shell-filling. The boundaries of most radiaxial structures are unconfined by shells (crossed polarizers).

An alternative explanation is the bodies of limestone do not constitute remnants of an intact bioherm but are parts of a now well-consolidated debris flow that originated on the shelf, was deposited in deep water in Silurian time, and finally was tectonically emplaced on Devonian rocks. This scheme seems unlikely because, as a debris flow, a great variety of rock types and age ranges would be expected, and these features were not observed.

The bioherm, if that is what it is, needs a more detailed description and comparison with the mudmound in southern Nevada and similar bodies in Newfoundland and Europe mentioned by Ross and others (1975).

Antler Orogenic Deposits

Nature of the Orogenic Sediments

The Harmony Formation, basal Havallah sequence of Silberling (1975) (see appendix, column 3), basal Inskip Formation, Grossman and Banner Formations, Bruffey sequence, and certain unnamed units are the subject of this discussion. These units, sometimes called the overlap assemblage, are at the base of a sequence of clastic deposits extending from Upper Devonian through the Mississippian to the lower part of the Pennsylvanian. Much of the material eroded from the Antler uplift in northern Nevada was deposited in shallow water on eastern facies carbonate rocks in the Antler foreland trough, outside the area described in this report (fig. 2, column 15). However, much also was deposited in deep water of the hinterland trough (columns 1–5) and in the shallow water of marine basins within the uplifted area (columns 7–14). Sandy arkosic turbidites and bouldery debris flows from a western source were pouring into the hinterland trough from the west in the same interval (Ketner and others, 2005). Small bodies of basaltic rocks (see appendix, columns 1, 3, 4, 7, and 9) and barite deposits (column 11) form part of the orogenic deposits, as they do in the western facies assemblage. Rhyolitic rocks, in addition to basalt, are present in the orogenic Inskip Formation of the East Range (Ketner, 2008).

Orogenic deposits within the area of the Antler uplift include coarse, clast-supported conglomerate derived from the western facies assemblage overlain by, or interbedded with, limestone. A fauna of bivalves and corals in some of the limestone (Nolan, 1933; Coats, 1987) indicates a shallow-marine environment.

In contrast, Antler orogenic deposits of the hinterland trough are notable for a scarcity of indigenous fauna and appear to be mainly debris flows and proximal turbidites characterized by chaotic bedding and relatively large angular clasts in a matrix of much finer grained material. The impression conveyed by these deposits is of unsorted sediments rapidly dumped into deep water. The following illustrations depict the sedimentary immaturity of these deposits, all of which are of Late Devonian to Early Mississippian age (figs. 18–28).

Figure 18. Harmony Formation, Hot Springs Range, a conglomeratic sandstone showing angular clast of granite (spanned by the yellow line); the mineral on the left side of the clast is quartz, that on the right is sericitized untwinned feldspar (crossed polarizers).

Figure 19. Harmony Formation, Hot Springs Range, illustrating the extreme angularity of many grains; large grains of quartz and untwinned feldspar in a matrix of quartz and feldspar (crossed polarizers).

Origin of the Orogenic Sediments

A large part of the orogenic sediments in the Hot Springs Range, East Range, Sonoma Range, Battle Mountain, and Osgood Mountains is composed of unsorted arkosic sediments and debris flows, some of which incorporate extremely large limestone boulders. All were derived from a terrane that must have been located just to the west as argued by Ketner and others (2005). Chert and quartzite clasts, however, compose a major part of the total orogenic clastic deposits. These, clearly

Figure 20.   Harmony Formation, Hot Springs Range , showing quartz and feldspar grains thickly strewn in limestone (crossed polarizers).

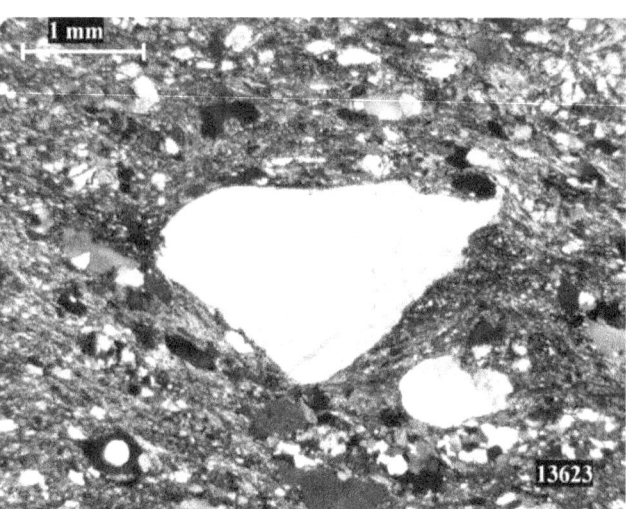

Figure 22.   Lower part of Inskip Formation, East Range, showing arkosic sandstone; large, angular quartz grain in finer grained matrix of quartz, feldspar, and mica (crossed polarizers).

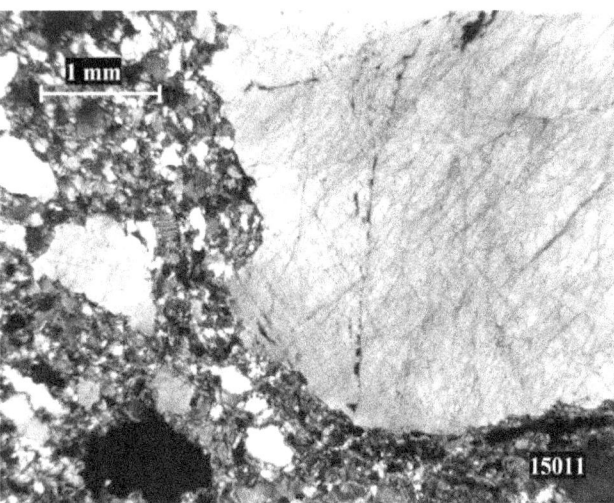

Figure 21.   Harmony Formation, Sonoma Range, showing large quartz grain in finer grained matrix of quartz and feldspar (crossed polarizers).

Figure 23.   Lower part of Inskip Formation, East Range, showing angular boulder of quartzite derived from the Valmy Formation in finer grained matrix. Vertical dimension of large clast about 10 cm.

Figure 24. Lower part of Inskip Formation, East Range, showing chert-grain conglomeratic sandstone with iron-oxide cement (crossed polarizers).

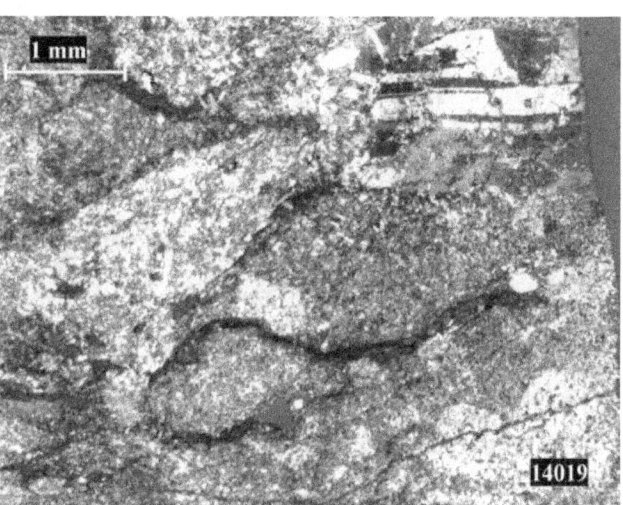

Figure 26. Clastic unit at the base of the Havallah sequence, Sonoma Range, showing angular chert-grain conglomeratic sandstone with feldspar grain in upper right (crossed polarizers).

Figure 25. Clastic unit at base of Havallah sequence, Sonoma Range. Quartzite cobbles derived from the Valmy Formation in a silty, sandy matrix.

Figure 27. Clastic unit at the base of the Havallah sequence, Sonoma Range, showing large quartz grain in matrix of finer grained quartz and chert (crossed polarizers).

derived from the western facies assemblage, were deposited not only in the hinterland and foreland troughs (fig. 2, columns 1–5 and 15) but also in shallow marine basins in the Antler highland area (fig. 2, columns 7–14).

The Valmy and Vinini Formations, the principal potential reservoirs of quartzite and chert clasts, are ubiquitous in the region and are shown in all but the last of the columns shown in figure 2. Where then was the source of the great volume of quartzite and chert clasts in the orogenic deposits? Two observations are pertinent. (1) In the northern Bull Run Mountains, northern Independence Mountains, and Rowland-Rosebud Mountain area, limestone beds just above the basal conglomerate are of Late Mississippian age, and in the same three

areas, the western facies assemblage has been eroded deeply into the Valmy Formation. The extensive area represented by these three localities could have been a major source of clastics in the Late Devonian and Early Mississippian. (2) In parts of the Bull Run and Osgood Mountains, Pennsylvanian beds lie unconformably on Cambrian rocks as noted in the appendix—the western facies assemblage has been completely eroded in these areas. Assuming that most of that erosion was of Antler age, the combined areas of partial and complete erosion of the Valmy Formation was probably adequate to account for the large volume of chert and quartzite clastics in the two troughs and in basins within the central highland area.

Figure 28. Clastic unit at the base of the Havallah sequence, Sonoma Range, showing large grain of strained quartz and rock chips in fine-grained matrix (crossed polarizers).

Antler Orogeny

The stratigraphic hiatus between the western facies rocks and the overlying Devonian to Mississippian orogenic deposits represents uplift and erosion during the Antler orogeny (fig. 2). The Antler orogeny consisted of regional uplift and did not involve tectonic emplacement of an allochthon. The following observations indicate the validity of this concept. (1) The depositional contact between the Valmy Formation, the essence of the western facies assemblage, and the underlying autochthonous Cambrian sedimentary sequence is clearly exposed in the East Range, northern Bull Run Mountains, and Rowland-Rosebud Mountain area (fig. 2). The precise locations where this contact can be observed in these areas, and in southern Nevada, are available in a previous publication (Ketner, 1998b). (2) Bedding in Devonian to Mississippian orogenic strata and underlying units of the western facies assemblage is clearly parallel in 10 mountain ranges in the area of this report and undetermined in four (fig. 2). This contact has been mapped in detail in the East Range (Whitebread, 1994), southern Independence Mountains (Ketner, 1998a), Adobe Range (Ketner and Ross, 1990), Rowland-Rosebud Mountain area (Ketner and others, 1995), HD Range (Riva, 1970), and Sulphur Spring Range (Carlisle and Nelson, 1990). In the East Range, the bedding above and below the contact is remarkably parallel for a distance of 20 km, and in most of these locations, the bedding is parallel over extensive areas. The significance of these disconformable relations in so many locations is the improbability that a sheet consisting of the western facies assemblage, the Roberts Mountains allochthon, could have been forced up the continental slope without strong deformation resulting in pervasive angular unconformities below the orogenic deposits. The complex structure now observed in the western facies assemblage and in the overlying orogenic deposits is due to multiple tectonic events occurring mainly between the Pennsylvanian and Miocene (Ketner, 1977, 1984, 1998b, 2012; Thorman and others, 1990; Ketner and Alpha, 1992; Trexler and others, 2004). (3) Conventional theories require an ocean basin or volcanic arc to the west of the western facies assemblage as indicated in the Introduction, but, in reality, a source of arkosic sediments and Cambrian limestone boulders lay to the west during the Antler orogeny (Ketner and others, 2005). (4) The lithic composition of the western facies assemblage is incompatible with an oceanic environment and proximity to a volcanic arc on which conventional theories of the Antler orogeny are based; for example, the presence of beds of pure quartzite and lack of an arc or of arc-derived sediments in the assemblage. (5) Rising sea level, rather than tectonism, can account for the deep-water aspects of the western facies assemblage such as dark color and lack of a shelly fauna. Rising sea level in the Cambrian is not an ad hoc concept but a well-established, long-standing fact (Sloss, 1963). (6) Finally, isolated exposures of shelf carbonates scattered in the western facies domain can be explained as slide blocks originating in collapse of the carbonate shelf, rather than as windows in an allochthon, as argued previously by Ketner (2012). This is an extension of a process observed in Alberta, Canada, where, in the Late Devonian, large blocks of shelf rocks have clearly spalled and slid far out into the western facies domain (Cook and others, 1972). Sandberg and others (1997) describe a similar process in southern Nevada. This process seems more credible than forcing a thin sheet of western facies rocks, composed largely of shale and chert, up the miogeoclinal ramp. Furthermore, many of the "windows" are mountain peaks towering over the surrounding western facies assemblage and, as many observers have remarked, more nearly resemble klippen or slide blocks than windows.

The Antler orogeny took place in the Devonian and Mississippian, but the precise age of its onset is uncertain. The majority of conodont collections from strata in the northern Adobe Range, southern Independence Mountains, and northern Sulphur Spring Range, considered to be the oldest orogenic deposits, indicate an early Late Devonian age. However, in the northern Adobe Range and the northern Sulphur Spring Range, a small number of conodont collections indicate a Middle Devonian age as noted in the appendix. Since the orogenic clastic sediments are redeposited, the anomalous Middle Devonian age could be due to reworking of the conodonts. Based on the data available, the age of the oldest orogenic deposits that have been accurately dated by means of conodonts is considered to be early Late Devonian and possibly Middle Devonian in some areas.

Conclusions

The stratigraphy of northern Nevada as described in this report is based, above all, on direct observation of relations in the field. The stratigraphy can be reconstructed based on presently known age data and observation of contacts. It is regionally consistent, and many stratigraphic details can be explained in terms of known regional changes in sea level—an allochthon is not required. With all its uncertainties, the stratigraphy reveals much about the nature and timing of the Antler orogeny—it involved regional uplift of part of the western facies assemblage, it began generally in the Late Devonian, and orogenic sediments were deposited in marine basins within the uplifted area as well as in peripheral troughs. The term "orogeny" customarily applied to this event is questionable because most of the classic features of mountain building are undocumented or clearly absent: folding, thrust faulting, metamorphism, involvement of basement rocks, and granitic plutonism.

In spite of all the work that has been done in the past 70 years, still more needs to be done—detailed mapping and much more paleontological data are required for a full understanding of the regional geologic history. Important issues remain to be investigated including (1) the role of contraction versus extension during the early to middle Paleozoic—elevation of the western facies assemblage suggests contraction, but the pervasive presence in Cambrian to Mississippian rocks of deep-seated greenstone and barite suggests extension; (2) exact ages, depositional environment, and source of the pure quartzite deposits; (3) detailed lithic composition of debris flows at the base of the Harmony Formation; (4) the present location of the provenance terrane of arkosic deposits and debris flows of the hinterland trough; (5) conditions surrounding chaotic sedimentation in the hinterland trough; and (6) the presence of igneous rocks and barite deposits in strata ranging from Cambrian to Mississippian and the presence of sulfide deposits in the western facies assemblage. Students looking for research projects should not assume that all the geologic problems in Nevada have been solved—many exciting opportunities remain.

Acknowledgments

Technical reviews by John E. Repetski, Christopher Holm-Denoma, and Thomas Judkins improved the manuscript and are greatly appreciated.

References Cited

Burchfiel, B.C., Cowan, D.S., and Davis, G.A., 1992, Tectonic overview of the Cordilleran orogen in the Western United States, *in* Burchfiel, B.C., Lipman, P.W., and Zoback, M.L., eds., The Cordilleran orogen—Conterminous U.S.: Boulder, Colo., Geological Society of America, Decade of North American Geology, The Geology of North America, v. G-3, p. 407–480.

Carlisle, Donald, and Nelson, C.A., 1990, Geologic map of the Mineral Hill quadrangle, Nevada: Nevada Bureau of Mines and Geology, Map 97, scale 1:48,000.

Coats, R.R., 1969, Upper Paleozoic formations of the Mountain City area, Elko County, Nevada, *in* Cohee, G.V., Bates, R.G., Wright B.W., eds., Contributions to stratigraphy, 1968: U.S. Geological Survey Bulletin 1274, p. A22–A27.

Coats, R.R., 1987, Geology of Elko County, Nevada: Nevada Bureau of Mines and Geology Bulletin 101, 112 p.

Cook, H.E., McDaniel, P.N., Mountjoy, E.W., and Pray, L.C., 1972, Allochthonous carbonate debris flows at Devonian bank ("reef") margins, Alberta, Canada: Bulletin of Canadian Petroleum Geology, v. 20, p. 439–497.

Crafford, A.E.J., 2007, Geologic map of Nevada: U.S. Geological Survey Data Series 249, scale 1:250,000, 1 CD-ROM, 46 p., 1 pl., available at http://pubs.usgs.gov/ds/2007/249/.

Crafford, A.E.J., 2008, Paleozoic tectonic domains of Nevada: An interpretive discussion to accompany the geologic map of Nevada: Geosphere, v. 4, no. 1, p. 260–291, doi: 10.1130/ GES00108.1.

Doebrich, J.L., 1994, Preliminary geologic map of the Galena Canyon quadrangle, Lander County, Nevada: U.S. Geological Survey Open-File Report 94–664, scale 1:24,000.

Ehman, K.D., 1985, Paleozoic stratigraphy and tectonics of the Bull Run Mountains, Elko County, northern Nevada: University of California, Davis, Ph.D. dissertation, 174 p.

Ferguson, H.G., Muller, S.W., and Roberts, R.J., 1951, Geologic map of the Winnemucca quadrangle, Nevada: U.S. Geological Survey Geologic Quadrangle Map GQ–11, scale 1:125,000.

Finney, S.C., and Perry, B.D., 1991, Depositional setting and paleogeography of Ordovician Vinini Formation, central Nevada, *in* Cooper, J.D., and Stevens, C.H., eds., 1991, Paleozoic paleogeography of the Western United States–II, Pacific Section: Society of Economic Paleontologists and Mineralogists, v. 67, p. 747–766.

Gilluly, James, 1967, Geologic map of the Winnemucca quadrangle, Pershing and Humboldt Counties, Nevada: U.S. Geological Survey Geological Quadrangle Map GQ–656, scale 1:62,500.

Gilluly, James, and Gates, Olcott, 1965, Tectonic and igneous geology of the northern Shoshone Range, Nevada: U.S. Geological Survey Professional Paper 465, 153 p.

Hotz, P.E., and Willden, Ronald, 1964, Geology and mineral deposits of the Osgood Mountains quadrangle, Humboldt County, Nevada: U.S. Geological Survey Professional Paper 431, 128 p.

Jones, A.E., 1997a, Geologic map of the Hot Springs Peak quadrangle and the southeastern part of the Little Poverty quadrangle, Nevada: Nevada Bureau of Mines and Geology Field Studies Map 14, scale 1:24,000.

Jones, A.E., 1997b, Geologic map of the Delvada Spring quadrangle, Nevada: Nevada Bureau of Mines and Geology Field Studies Map 13, scale 1:24,000.

Ketner, K.B., 1966, Comparison of Ordovician eugeosynclinal and miogeosynclinal quartzites of the cordilleran geosyncline: U.S. Geological Survey Professional Paper 550–C, p. C54–C60.

Ketner, K.B., 1977, Late Paleozoic orogeny and sedimentation, southern California, Nevada, Idaho, and Montana, *in* Stewart, J.H., Stevens, C.H., and Fritsche, A.E., eds., 1977, Paleozoic paleogeography of the Western United States, Symposium–I, Pacific Section: Society of Economic Paleontologists and Mineralogists, p. 363–369.

Ketner, K.B., 1980, Stratigraphic and tectonic parallels between Paleozoic geosynclinal siliceous sequences in northern Nevada and those of the Marathon uplift, Texas, and Ouachita Mountains, Arkansas and Oklahoma, *in* Fouch, T.D., and Magathan, E.R., eds., Paleozoic paleogeography of west-central United States, Symposium 1, June 1980, Rocky Mountain Section, Denver, Colorado: Society of Economic Paleontologists and Mineralogists, p. 363–366.

Ketner, K.B., 1983, Strata-bound, silver-bearing, iron, lead, and zinc sulfide deposits in Silurian and Ordovician rocks of allochthonous terranes, Nevada and northern Mexico: U.S. Geological Survey Open-File Report 83–792, 7 p.

Ketner, K.B., 1984, Recent studies indicate that major structures in northeastern Nevada and the Golconda thrust in north-central Nevada are of Jurassic or Cretaceous age: Geology, v. 12, p. 483–486.

Ketner, K.B., 1991, Stratigraphy and strata-bound lead-zinc-barium mineralization of lower Paleozoic western-facies rocks in northeastern Nevada, *in* Raines, G.L., Lisle, R.E., Schafer, R.W., and Wilkinson, W.H., eds., Geology and ore deposits of the Great Basin, Symposium Proceedings, Reno, Nevada, April 1–5, 1990: Geological Society of Nevada, p. 539–551.

Ketner, K.B., 1998a, Geologic map of the Southern Independence Mountains, Elko County, Nevada: U.S. Geological Survey Miscellaneous Investigations Series Map I–2629, scale 1:24,000.

Ketner, K.B., 1998b, The nature and timing of tectonism in the western facies terrane of Nevada and California—An outline of evidence and interpretations derived from geologic maps of key areas: U.S. Geological Survey Professional Paper 1592, 19 p.

Ketner, K.B., 2007, Geologic map of the Gold Creek gold district, Elko County, Nevada: U.S. Geological Survey Scientific Investigations Map 2992, scale 1:24,000.

Ketner, K.B., 2008, The Inskip Formation, the Harmony Formation, and the Havallah sequence of northwestern Nevada—An interrelated Paleozoic assemblage in the home of the Sonoma orogeny: U.S. Geological Survey Professional Paper 1757, 20 p.

Ketner, K.B., 2012, An alternative hypothesis for the mid-Paleozoic Antler orogeny in Nevada: U.S. Geological Survey Professional Paper 1790, 11 p., available at *http://pubs.usgs.gov/pp/1790/*.

Ketner, K.B., and Alpha, A.G., 1992, Mesozoic and Tertiary rocks near Elko, Nevada—Evidence for Jurassic to Eocene folding and low-angle faulting: U.S. Geological Survey Bulletin 1988–C, p. C1–C13.

Ketner, K.B., Crafford, A.E.J., Harris, A.G., Repetski, J.E., and Wardlaw, B.R., 2005, Late Devonian to Mississippian arkosic rock derived from a granitic terrane in northwestern Nevada adds a new dimension to the Antler orogeny, *in* Rhoden, H.N., Steininger, R.C., and Vikre, P.G., eds., Geological Society of Nevada Symposium 2005: Window to the World, Reno, Nevada, May 2005: Geological Society of Nevada, p. 135–145.

Ketner, K.B., Day, W.C., Elrick, Maya, Vaag, M.K., Zimmermann, R.A., Snee, L.W., Saltus, R.W., Repetski, J.E., Wardlaw, B.R., Taylor, M.E., and Harris, A.G., 1998, An outline of tectonic, igneous, and metamorphic events in the Goshute-Toano Range between Silver Zone Pass and White Horse Pass, Elko County, Nevada: A history of superposed contractional and extensional deformation: U.S. Geological Survey Professional Paper 1593, 12 p.

Ketner, K.B., Ehman, K.D., Repetski, J.E., Stamm, R.G., and Wardlaw, B.R., 1993, Paleozoic stratigraphy and tectonics in northernmost Nevada: Implications for the nature of the Antler orogeny [abs.]: Geological Society of America Abstracts with Programs, v. 25, no. 5, p. 62.

Ketner, K.B., and Noll, J.H., Jr., 1987, Preliminary geologic map of the Cerro Cobachi area, Sonora, Mexico: U.S. Geological Survey Miscellaneous Field Studies Map MF–1980, scale 1:20,000.

Ketner, K.B., Repetski, J.E., Wardlaw, B.R., and Stamm, R.C., 1995, Geologic map of the Rowland-Bearpaw Mountain area, Elko County, Nevada: U.S. Geological Survey Miscellaneous Investigations Series Map I–2536, scale 1:24,000.

Ketner, K.B., and Ross, R.J., Jr., 1990, Geologic map of the northern Adobe Range, Elko County, Nevada: U.S. Geological Survey Miscellaneous Investigations Series Map I–2081, scale 1:24,000.

Ketner, K.B., Wardlaw, B.R., Harris, A.G., and Repetski, J.E., 2000, The East Range, northwestern Nevada-A neglected key to the tectonic history of the region, in Cluer, J.K., Price, J.G., Struhsacker, E.M., Hardyman, R.F., and Morris, C.L., eds., Geology and ore deposits 2000—The Great Basin and beyond: Geological Society of Nevada Symposium Proceedings, May 15–18, 2000, p. 389–396.

King, P.B., 1937, Geology of the Marathon region, Texas: U.S. Geological Survey Professional Paper 187, 148 p.

Lochman-Balk, Christina, 1972, Cambrian System, in Mallory, W.W., ed., Geologic atlas of the Rocky Mountain region: Rocky Mountain Association of Geologists, p. 60–75.

McCollum, L.B., and McCollum, Michael, 1991, Paleozoic rocks of the Osgood Mountains, Nevada, in Raines, G.L., Lisle, R.E., Schafer, R.W., and Wilkinson, W.H., eds., Geology and ore deposits of the Great Basin, Symposium Proceedings, Geological Society of Nevada, Reno, Nevada: Geological Society of Nevada, p. 735–738.

McCollum, L.B., and Miller D.M., 1991, Cambrian stratigraphy of the Wendover area, Utah and Nevada: U.S. Geological Survey Bulletin 1948, 43 p.

Miller, E.L., Holdsworth, B.K., Whiteford, W.B., and Rodgers, D., 1984, Stratigraphy and structure of the Schoonover sequence, northeastern Nevada: Implications for Paleozoic plate-margin tectonics: Geological Society of America Bulletin, v. 95, p. 1063–1076.

Miller, E.L., and Larue, D.K., 1983, Ordovician quartzite in the Roberts Mountains allochthon, Nevada: Deep sea fan deposits derived from cratonal North America, in Stevens, C.H., ed., Pre-Jurassic rocks in Cordilleran allochthonous terranes: Society of Economic Paleontologists and Mineralogists, Pacific Section, Special Publication, p. 91–102.

Miller, E.L., Miller, M.M., Stevens, C.H., Wright, J.E., and Madrid, Raul, 1992, Late Paleozoic paleogeographic and tectonic evolution of the Western U.S. Cordillera, in Burchfiel, B.C., Lipman, P.W., and Zoback, M.L., eds., The Cordilleran orogen: Conterminous U.S.: Boulder, Colo., Geological Society of America, The Geology of North America, v. G–3, p. 57–106.

Noble, P.J., 1994, Silurian radiolarian zonation for the Caballos Novaculite, Marathon uplift, west Texas: Bulletin of American Paleontology 106 (345), p. 1–55.

Noble, P.J., 2000, Revised stratigraphy and structural relationships in the Roberts Mountains allochthon of Nevada (USA) based on radiolarian cherts, in Cluer, J.K., Price, J.G., Stuhsacker, E.M., Hardyman, R.F., and Morris, C.L., eds., Geology and ore deposits 2000: The Great Basin and beyond, Geological Society of Nevada Symposium Proceedings, May 15–18, 2000: Geological Society of Nevada, p. 439–449.

Noble, P.J., and Finney, S.C., 1999, Recognition of fine-scale imbricate thrusts in lower Paleozoic orogenic belts—An example from the Roberts Mountains allochthon, Nevada: Geology, v. 27, no. 6, p. 543–546.

Noble, P.J., Ketner, K.B., and McClellan, W., 1997, Early Silurian radiolaria from northern Nevada, USA: Marine Micropaleontology, v. 30, p. 215–223.

Nolan, T.B., circa 1933, The Mountain City mining district, Elko County, Nevada: U.S. Geological Survey informal report: U.S. Geological Survey library designation (200) N642m, 30 p.

Nolan, T.B., Merriam, C.W., and Williams, J.S., 1956, The stratigraphic section in the vicinity of Eureka, Nevada: U.S. Geological Survey Professional Paper 276, 76 p.

Oversby, Brian, 1972, Thrust sequences in the Windermere Hills, northeastern Elko County, Nevada: Geological Society of America Bulletin, v. 83, p. 2677–2688.

Poole, F.G., Stewart, J.H., Palmer, A.R., Sandberg, C.A., Madrid, R.J., Ross, R.J., Jr., Hintze, L.F., Miller, M.M., and Wrucke, C.T., 1992, Latest Precambrian to latest Devonian time: Development of a continental margin, in Burchfiel, B.C., Lipman, P.W., and Zoback, M.L., eds., The Cordilleran orogen: Conterminous U.S.: Boulder, Colo., Geological Society of America, The Geology of North America, v. G–3, p. 9–56.

Rees, M.N., and Rowell, A.J., 1980, Preble Formation, a Cambrian outer continental shelf deposit in Nevada: Provo, Utah, Brigham Young University Geology Studies, v. 27, part 1, p. 1–8.

Riva, John, 1970, Thrusted Paleozoic rocks in the northern and central HD Range, northeastern Nevada: Geological Society of America Bulletin, v. 81, p. 2689–2716.

Riva, John, and Ketner, K.B., 1989, Ordovician graptolites from the northern Sierra de Cobachi, Sonora, Mexico: Transactions of the Royal Society of Edinburgh, Earth Sciences, no. 80, p. 71–90.

Roberts, R.J., 1964, Stratigraphy and structure of the Antler Peak quadrangle, Humboldt and Lander Counties, Nevada: U.S. Geological Survey Professional Paper 459–A, 93 p.

Ross, R.J., Jr., Jaanusson, Valdar, and Friedman, Irving, 1975, Lithology and origin of Middle Ordovician calcareous mudmound at Meiklejohn Peak, southern Nevada: U.S. Geological Survey Professional Paper 871, 48 p.

Sandberg, C.A., Morrow, J.R., and Warme, J.E., 1997, Late Devonian Alamo impact event, Global Kellwasser events and major eustatic events, eastern Great Basin, Nevada and Utah: Provo, Utah, Brigham Young University Geology Studies, v. 42, part I, p. 129–160.

Seeland, D.A., 1968, Paleo-currents of the Late Precambrian to Early Ordovician (basal Sauk) transgressive clastics of the western and northern United States with a review of the stratigraphy: Salt Lake City, University of Utah, Ph.D. dissertation, 276 p.

Silberling, N.J., 1975, Age relationships of the Golconda thrust fault, Sonoma Range, north-central Nevada: Geological Society of America Special Paper 163, 28 p.

Sloss, S.L., 1963, Sequences in the cratonic interior of North America: Geological Society of America Bulletin 74, p. 93–114.

Smith, J.F., Jr., and Ketner, K.B., 1978, Geologic map of the Carlin-Piñon Range area, Elko and Eureka Counties, Nevada: U.S. Geological Survey Miscellaneous Investigations Series Map I–1028, scale 1:62,500.

Stewart, J.H., 1980, Geology of Nevada: A discussion to accompany the Geologic Map of Nevada: Nevada Bureau of Mines and Geology Special Publication 4, 136 p.

Stewart, J.H., and Carlson, 1978, Geologic map of Nevada: U.S. Geological Survey, scale 1:500,000.

Theodore, T.G., 1994, Preliminary geologic map of the Snow Gulch quadrangle, Humboldt and Lander Counties, Nevada: U.S Geological Survey Open-File Report 94–436, scale 1:24,000.

Thorman, C.H., Ketner, K.B., Brooks, W.E., Snee, L.W., and Zimmermann, R.A., 1990, Late Mesozoic-Cenozoic tectonics in northeastern Nevada, *in* Raines, G.L., Lisle, R.E., Schafer, R.W., and Wilkinson, W.H., eds., Geology and ore deposits of the Great Basin: Geological Society of Nevada Symposium Proceedings, v. 2, p. 25–45.

Trexler, J.H., Cashman, P.H., Snyder, W.S., and Davydov, V.I., 2004, Late Paleozoic tectonism in Nevada: Timing, kinematics, and tectonic significance: Geological Society of America Bulletin, v. 116, p. 525–538.

Whitebread, D.H., 1994, Geologic map of the Dun Glen quadrangle, Pershing County, Nevada: U.S. Geological Survey Miscellaneous Investigations Series Map I–2409, scale 1:48,000.

Appendix

Appendix. Stratigraphic Columns of Figure 2

The columns are an attempt to extract the original stratigraphic sequences from fragments isolated by faults. Good evidence supports these interpretations in the form of paleontological age data and direct observation of original sedimentary contacts; these are shown as heavy lines in figure 2. Location numbers corresponding to those in the column headings are shown in figure 1. The strata included in these columns are clustered mainly at two stratigraphic levels: Cambrian to Middle Silurian and Upper Devonian to Mississippian. The clusters are separated by an erosional hiatus that represents the Antler orogeny.

Column 1. Hot Springs Range

This column is based primarily on mapping by Jones (1997a,b) as interpreted by Ketner and others (2005) and Ketner (2008). In this interpretation, the chert part of the "Cambrian" Paradise Valley Chert of Jones is a regional chert couplet consisting of a lower black chert unit and an upper white chert unit, which sits at the boundary between the Ordovician and Silurian. The upper part of the couplet is the Lower Silurian Cherry Spring chert of Noble and others (1997); the lower part is Upper Ordovician. The couplet is here included in the Valmy Formation. The limestone part of the Paradise Valley Chert consists of large boulders and slabs of Cambrian limestone in debris flows at the base of the Upper Devonian to Lower Mississippian Harmony Formation. This hiatus, within the Paradise Valley Chert, between the Lower Silurian part of the Valmy Formation and Upper Devonian to Mississippian Harmony Formation represents the Antler orogeny (see Ketner and others, 2005, for data on age of the Harmony Formation). The term Paradise Valley Chert is obsolete and here abandoned for the reasons stated above. Above the Harmony Formation are Mississippian units bearing basaltic and rhyolitic rocks that are similar to those of the Inskip Formation in the East Range.

Column 2. Osgood Mountains

Column 2 is derived from mapping by Hotz and Willden (1964) supplemented by information on the Preble Formation by Rees and Rowell (1980). It includes age data on the Goughs Canyon and Farrel Canyon Formations supplied by Jones, cited in Ketner and others (2005), and by McCollum and McCollum (1991). As assembled in this column, the sequence in the Osgood Mountains resembles that of the neighboring Hot Springs, Sonoma, and East Ranges. In all three of these ranges, the Valmy Formation is overlain disconformably by a chaotic assemblage of igneous and sedimentary rocks including arkosic sandstone and basaltic rocks (Ketner, 2008), all

of which can be found in either the Goughs Canyon or Farrel Canyon Formations.

In one area of the Osgood Mountains—not shown on figure 2—upper Paleozoic rocks lie unconformably on Cambrian strata. This profound hiatus represents both the mid-Pennsylvanian Humboldt orogeny of Ketner (1977), events described by Trexler and others (2004), and the Antler orogeny. The term Osgood Mountain Quartzite is used in this column for clarity rather than the equivalent Prospect Mountain Quartzite, but the latter has priority and the name Osgood Mountain is superfluous. Though formally named by Hotz and Willden (1964), strata mapped as Goughs Canyon and Farrel Canyon Formations require much more study to confirm their classification as formal stratigraphic units.

Column 3. Sonoma Range

This column is based on mapping by Gilluly (1967) and Silberling (1975) and on my observations in Clear Creek (Clear Water on some maps), Bacon, and Grand Trunk Canyons—adjacent canyons in the area mapped by Silberling. Column 3 is a composite that draws on contact relations displayed in one or another of the three canyons. In Clear Creek Canyon, parts of the Preble and Valmy Formations are exposed. Although their contact is obscure, they are assumed to have been in sequence originally, as they are in the neighboring East Range (Ketner and others, 2000). In Bacon Canyon, the middle to upper part of the Valmy Formation, including the chert couplet at its stratigraphic top, is well exposed and is overlain disconformably by the Harmony Formation.

In both Clear Creek and Grand Trunk Canyons, the Valmy Formation is overlain by the "clastic unit of the Havallah sequence" of Silberling (1975) as shown in figure 12. The clastic unit is Upper Devonian and Lower Mississippian (Ketner and others, 2000) and therefore appears to be a facies of the Harmony Formation. However, the clastic unit is generally more coarse grained and contains a much smaller proportion of feldspar. The disconformity between the Valmy Formation and overlying Harmony Formation (or clastic unit) represents the Antler orogeny. The Osgood Mountain Quartzite, which normally underlies the Preble, is not exposed in the area mapped by Silberling but is present elsewhere in the Sonoma Range (Gilluly, 1967).

Column 4. East Range

Column 4 was derived primarily from the geologic map of part of the East Range by Whitebread (1994) and additional data by Ketner and others (2000) and Ketner (2008). The contact between the Cambrian Preble Formation and the overlying Valmy Formation is depositional and gradational as observed in outcrops. One of the more accessible exposures of this contact is 4 km east of Kyle Hot Springs (for location of Kyle Hot Springs see Stewart and Carlson, 1978). On most published geologic maps, the Preble of the East Range is misdated as Triassic and its contact with the overlying Ordovician rocks is necessarily shown as a fault parallel with bedding (for example, Ferguson and others, 1951; Stewart and Carlson, 1978). The fault is no longer necessary because the age of upper beds in the "Triassic" formation are close to the Cambrian-Ordovician boundary as determined by conodont collections (J.E. Repetski, cited in Ketner and others, 2000).

The contact between the middle part of the Valmy Formation and the overlying Upper Devonian(?) to Mississippian beds of the Inskip Formation is a disconformity as indicated by abundant parallel bedding attitudes in both units along a well-exposed contact 20 km long. The hiatus represents the Antler orogeny. The Inskip is extremely heterogeneous, but arkosic sandstone, greenstone, and rhyolitic rocks constitute a large proportion. The precise age of the base of the Inskip is uncertain. Well-dated beds far above the base are of late Early Mississippian age and one collection could be as old as Late Devonian (Ketner and others, 2000). The geologic map of Whitebread (1994) indicates that the Cambrian to Upper Triassic stratigraphic sequence in the East Range is nearly concordant throughout, and although there is clearly a stratigraphic gap between the Valmy and Inskip Formations, the sequence displays no structural evidence of intense deformation of any age prior to the Jurassic.

Column 5. Battle Mountain

Column 5 is based on mapping by Roberts (1964), Doebrich (1994), and Theodore (1994), and on my observations. The "Cambrian" Scott Canyon Formation of Roberts (1964) is here divided between the Ordovician to Lower Silurian Valmy Formation and the Upper Devonian to Mississippian Harmony Formation as detailed previously (Ketner, 2008). The original assignment of the Scott Canyon to the Cambrian was based on Cambrian fossils in limestone "lenses" in the formation. These lenses actually are very large boulders or slabs in debris flows at the base of the Harmony Formation (Ketner, 2008). Because the name Scott Canyon was misapplied to rocks that are actually part of the Valmy and Harmony Formations, I herein abandon the name.

Column 6. Northern Shoshone Range

As mapped, few of the relevant contacts in the northern Shoshone Range are depositional (Gilluly and Gates, 1965). Therefore, the stratigraphic units are assembled on the basis of their ages and stratigraphic relations where they are better exposed in other mountain ranges. According to Gilluly and Gates, the Prospect Mountain Quartzite is topped by shaley beds that they identified as the Pioche Shale. The Eldorado Dolomite is assumed to have been originally in depositional sequence with the shaley beds, as in eastern Nevada (Nolan and others, 1956). The Shwin Formation of the northern Shoshone Range is equivalent to the Preble Formation of the Osgood Mountains area and, in part, to the Tennessee

Mountain Formation in more northern exposures. In the present interpretation, the Shwin or Preble Formation originally overlay the Eldorado depositionally, and was overlain depositionally by the Valmy Formation as in the East Range. The Elder Sandstone occupies most of the Silurian (and the Lower Devonian according to Noble, 2000). Conodonts (Anna Dombrowski, Univ. of Kansas, written commun., 1977) and radiolarians (Noble, 2000) from the Slaven Chert indicate its age ranges from Middle to Late Devonian, confirming the age range cited by Gilluly and Gates (1965). The Harmony Formation is exposed in a small area among units regarded by Gilluly and Gates as being exotic with respect to the Shoshone Range; all of these units are here considered to be a part of the local stratigraphic sequence for reasons detailed previously (Ketner, 1998b). As the stratigraphic sequence is assembled here, there is little evidence, in the form of a stratigraphic gap, of the Antler orogeny prior to the Mississippian.

The Valmy Formation, Elder Sandstone, and Slaven Chert are extremely heterogeneous aggregations defined principally by their ages as determined by sparse paleontological data. Because their thicknesses, internal stratigraphy, and stratigraphic limits are unknown, and they are not mappable units strictly on the basis of their lithic composition, they need further study to verify their status as formal formation-rank units.

Column 7. Northern Bull Run Mountains

This column is based on relations as mapped by Ehman (1985) and on reinterpretations developed in the field by Ehman and me (Ketner and others, 1993). According to these interpretations, the Edgemont Formation is the correlative of the Pioche Shale of the eastern shelf area (Nolan and others, 1956). The Bull Run Dolomite is the correlative of the Eldorado Dolomite of the eastern shelf area and the northern Shoshone Range. The combined Aura and Van Duzer Formations of Ehman, composed largely of calcareous turbidite, is partly equivalent to the Tennessee Mountain Formation. It is overlain by the Valmy Formation with a gradational, depositional contact (Ketner and others, 1993; Ketner, 1998b). The contact is well exposed on the ridge that extends northward from the peak of Pennsylvania Hill where it is gradational for a stratigraphic interval of 30 m (for location of Pennsylvania Hill, see Coats, 1987).

In the Rio Tinto area, at the extreme northern end of the range, the Valmy Formation is overlain by a sequence including a basal conglomerate (Grossman Formation), limestone (Banner Formation), and basalt (Nelson Formation) (Coats, 1987). Because they are interbedded in places, the units that overlie the Valmy are essentially the same age. The Banner contains fossils of early Late Mississippian age (Coats, 1987).

The stratigraphic gap between the Valmy Formation and the Grossman Formation represents the Antler orogeny. The contact between the Valmy and the Grossman has been declared to be "essentially conformable" (Nolan, 1933) and an "angular unconformity" (Coats, 1969). I tend to agree with Nolan, but the issue needs more attention. In nearby areas the contact is disconformable (fig. 2, columns 8 and 9).

In part of the Bull Run Mountains—not shown on fig. 2—the Pennsylvanian Porter Peak Formation of Ehman (1985), a local conglomeratic unit, lies directly on Cambrian rocks with a depositional contact. This profound angular unconformity represents the mid-Pennsylvanian Humboldt orogeny of Ketner (1977), events described by Trexler and others (2004), and the Antler orogeny.

Column 8. Northern Independence Mountains

Column 8 is based on mapping in the Schoonover Creek area by Miller and others (1984) and on my observations. On the divide between Schoonover Creek and Coffin Creek, the Valmy Formation is overlain with a well-exposed disconformable contact by conglomerate and Upper Mississippian limestone, here assigned to the Grossman and Banner Formations of Coats (1969, 1987). For locations of Schoonover and Coffin Creeks, see Miller and others (1984). The disconformity represents the Antler orogeny.

Column 9. Rowland-Rosebud Mountain Area

This column is based on geologic maps by Ketner and others (1995) and Ketner (2007). The Paleozoic rocks in the Rowland-Rosebud Mountain area in extreme northern Nevada are assumed originally to have formed an intact stratigraphic sequence from Lower Cambrian to Permian. However, this original continuity is now divided into two segments by a large granitic stock (Coats, 1987) and is sliced by high-angle faults in the Pennsylvanian and Permian part (Ketner and others, 1995). At Rosebud Mountain, the Cambrian Prospect Mountain Quartzite is overlain by the Cambrian to Ordovician Tennessee Mountain Formation, primarily a calcareous turbidite, with a concordant, depositional contact (Ketner, 2007). Basal beds of the Tennessee Mountain are similar to the Edgemont Formation of Ehman (1985). Conodont collections indicate that upper beds of the Tennessee Mountain exposed in the Rowland-Rosebud Mountain area are of Early and Middle Ordovician age (J.E. Repetski cited in Ketner and others, 1995). These upper beds are overlain depositionally and concordantly by the Valmy Formation. A good exposure of this contact is just south of Trail Gulch where both units are well dated (Ketner and others, 1995). The Valmy is overlain disconformably by conglomerate and upper Lower to Upper Mississippian limestone (Ketner and others, 1995)—equivalent to the Grossman and Banner Formations of Coats (1969, 1987). The disconformity, exposed just south of Rowland, represents the Antler orogeny.

The Tennessee Mountain and Preble Formations are essentially the same unit, but a case can be made for retention of both names because upper beds of the type Tennessee Mountain are of mid-Ordovician age, whereas those of the Preble Formation are at the Cambrian-Ordovician boundary (Ketner and others, 2000).

Column 10. Northern Adobe Range

This column represents relations near Badger Spring where unnamed Upper Devonian conglomerate, sandstone, limestone, and shale overlie remnants of the Silurian Elder Formation and the Vinini Formation disconformably (Ketner and Ross, 1990). The great majority of fossil collections indicate a Late Devonian age for the unnamed rocks. However, one small cluster of closely spaced conodont collections indicates both a Late and Middle Devonian age. I suspect the Middle Devonian conodonts were reworked; more data are needed. This hiatus represents the Antler orogeny. Elsewhere in the range, Permian rocks overlie Silurian strata unconformably representing the mid-Pennsylvanian Humboldt orogeny of Ketner (1977), events described by Trexler and others (2004), and the Antler orogeny.

Column 11. Southern Independence Mountains

The Vinini Formation, including the Ordovician-Silurian chert couplet at its stratigraphic top, is overlain conformably by Middle Silurian siltstone and sandstone (Elder Sandstone), which are overlain disconformably by unnamed strata of Late Devonian age (Ketner, 1998a). The Devonian beds are composed of conglomerate, limestone, chert, sandstone, greenstone, and bedded barite. The conglomerate includes pebbles composed partly of *Nuia*, an alga of Late Cambrian to Early Ordovician age, indicating erosion down to that level at some nearby location. The disconformity represents the Antler orogeny.

Column 12. Northern Piñon Range

This column is based on mapping by Smith and Ketner (1978). The Vinini Formation is present in two areas of the Piñon Range. Column 12 represents the northern exposure where the stratigraphic relations appear to be relatively uncomplicated. Here the Vinini is overlain by Mississippian units including, successively, Webb Formation, Chainman Shale, and Diamond Peak Formation. The youngest dated beds of the Vinini in this area are of early Late Ordovician age; the oldest overlying beds are early Early Mississippian. The gap represents the Antler orogeny.

Column 13. Northern Sulphur Spring Range

Column 13 is based on mapping by Smith and Ketner (1978), Carlisle and Nelson (1990), and my recent observations. In the northern Sulphur Spring Range, the Vinini Formation includes a thin (50 m) quartzite-bearing sequence of Ordovician age, which was, in retrospect, improperly termed the Valmy Formation by Smith and Ketner (1978). Carlisle and Nelson followed this questionable usage of the term in their map of the Mineral Hill quadrangle (1990). This thin unit, the "Valmy Formation," is overlain disconformably by the informally named "Bruffey sequence" of Devonian age. The Bruffey is an Antler orogenic sequence of boulder conglomerate composed largely of chert clasts and overlying graded calcarenite beds. Conodonts from the calcarenite range in age from Middle to Late Devonian. The oldest conodonts derived from the calcarenite beds are early Middle Devonian (Anna Dombrowski, Univ. of Kansas, written commun., 1977). If that were the true age of the strata, they would be among the oldest known Antler orogenic deposits. However, the calcarenite is redeposited, and therefore, the Bruffey beds may be somewhat younger than the dated conodonts; a more intensive study is needed. In any case, Upper Ordovician, Silurian, and Lower Devonian beds are missing. The parallelism of beds above and below the contact between the thin Ordovician quartzite-bearing unit and the overlying Devonian beds, over an extensive area, as mapped by Carlisle and Nelson (1990), reveals a complete absence of deformation in that interval. Nowhere does the Bruffey sequence lie on any other unit. The disconformity represents the Antler orogeny.

Column 14. HD Range

This column is based on mapping by Riva (1970) and my observations in his map area. In Riva's nomenclature, the oldest units in the HD Range are the Ordovician Valder Formation and Tiser Limestone. These constitute a sequence that is similar to parts of the lower and middle members of the Vinini Formation as described in the present report. The Agort Chert of Riva (1970) is Upper Ordovician dark, bedded chert, some beds of which are unusually thick. The Silurian Noh Formation consists of two units, a lower thick-bedded white chert and an upper micaceous siltstone unit. The white chert unit is here correlated with the Lower Silurian Cherry Spring chert of Noble and others (1997), and the siltstone unit is Middle Silurian. The combined Ordovician Agort Chert and Lower Silurian white chert is the chert couplet at the Ordovician-Silurian boundary exposed widely in Nevada and beyond. The formation names Valder, Tiser, Agort, and Noh are used only in the HD Range and nearby Windermere Hills (Oversby, 1972).

In the HD Range, wherever the stratigraphic base of the Mississippian Diamond Peak Formation is exposed, and it is exposed extensively, it overlies the same unit—the Ordovician Agort Chert, according to Riva's map. Nowhere does the Diamond Peak lie depositionally on any other unit. This disconformity testifies to regional uplift and erosion without local deformation in the interval between Ordovician and Mississippian.

Column 15. Goshute-Toano Range

Column 15, representing the eastern margin of the foreland trough, is based on stratigraphic studies of the Cambrian by McCollum and Miller (1991) and the Ordovician to Mississippian stratigraphic summary of Ketner and others (1998). The sequence between the Lower to Middle Cambrian shales and the Upper Devonian to Mississippian Pilot Shale is composed almost entirely of shallow-water limestone and dolomite—the carbonate shelf. The Pilot Shale, Chainman Shale, and Diamond Peak Formation constitute Antler orogenic sediments deposited in stratigraphic continuity with underlying carbonate rocks of the shelf. The Antler orogeny here is indicated solely by the arrival of siliceous sediments derived from the western facies assemblage.